A Wisle

Reclaiming the Neglected Garden

DENNIS WOODLAND

Cassell

The Royal Horticultural Society

THE ROYAL HORTICULTURAL SOCIETY

Cassell Educational Limited
Villiers House, 41/47 Strand,
London WC2N 5JE
for the Royal Horticultural Society

First published 1991

British Library Cataloguing in Publication Data
Woodland, Dennis 1924–
  Reclaiming the neglected garden.
  1. Gardening
  I. Title   II. Series
  635

  ISBN 0-304-31966-X

Photographs on pages 4, 15, 27 (left) and 32 by Michael
Warren. All other photographs by the author

Line drawings by Mike Shoebridge

Typeset by Chapterhouse Ltd, Formby
Printed in Hong Kong by Wing King Tong Co. Ltd

Front cover: So often a mature garden can become
overgrown if neglected for a single season. This garden,
with a paved sitting area and half-barrel planted with a
hydrangea, has an atmosphere of seclusion and
luxuriance
Frontispiece: A scree garden is a delightful feature, but
once it has been established make sure it is kept weed-
free
Back cover: A neglected garden, overgrown and ready
for reclamation
  photograph by Michael Warren

Contents

Introduction

When a property changes hands, the garden often suffers a period of neglect – from two or three months to several years – during which perhaps the lawn has been mown but little else done to control weeds or prune trees, shrubs or climbers. The subject of this book, therefore, highlights a situation which faces many of us when we move house. Whatever the reasons for neglect, the prospect of garden restoration can be somewhat daunting and, as a result, much of the garden work tends to be left for a year or so, during which further deterioration sets in. Improvement to the house inevitably has greater importance for most people and the budget may not extend to calling in professionals for the garden as well as the house!

In the following pages, I suggest an order of priority and offer advice on dealing with the tasks and problems likely to be encountered by the owner of the small or medium-sized neglected garden. 'How long will it take?' is a question I am often asked. Of course, so much depends on the size of the garden and the extent of the neglect, and on whether you wish to do all the work yourself or with some help from local landscapers. However, in the average small garden, you will find that, apart from structural repairs or additions, it should be possible to make a start with weed-killing or clearance in early autumn; to follow this with manure-spreading, rotovation and/or hand digging, given three or four fine weekends in October and November; to resite some larger existing shrubs during open weather in December; and, allowing for settling of manured and cultivated areas, to have the garden ready for replanting with young transplants or container-grown stock (perhaps another one or two weekends) in early spring. It will certainly be practical, with a fine autumn, to prepare ground and sow grass seed during October and to see the beginnings of a reasonable lawn by the following spring.

A garden showing the classic signs of neglect: the grass is becoming tussocky and stinging nettles have invaded the borders

Overcoming Weeds

Almost universal constituents of long-neglected gardens are such persistent perennial weeds as bramble, stinging nettle, couch grass, horsetail, bindweed, ground elder, dock and dandelion. These can seriously inhibit any new planting. A priority task when taking over a neglected garden is to assess the degree of infestation, giving thought at this stage to the main features you want to initiate or maintain in the garden and how they relate to weed-infested parts. For example, you may wish to install a patio or gravel path or to site a conservatory over an area heavily infested with dock, dandelion or horsetail, all of which will grow through tarmacadam and the smallest gaps in paving. In this instance, it would be preferable to use a total weedkiller with a systemic action – amitrole (aminotriazole) with simazine or MCPA – rather than to dig or rotovate the ground, where disturbance may cause future subsidence.

HERBACEOUS BORDERS

A familiar problem is the herbaceous border which has become heavily infested with ground elder. Here, it is usually best to start again. In autumn or spring, remove small clumps of valued plants, carefully disentangling the white roots of ground elder before temporarily laying-in the plants in a convenient corner of the vegetable garden, or accommodating them in deep trays or boxes of soil, to await replanting; do not forget to label the clumps. The weedy border may then be treated with the efficient non-persistent systemic herbicide glyphosate, repeating the applications if necessary. This is best applied from April to August, when the vegetation is growing vigorously, as it will act more rapidly and there will be plenty of green top growth to absorb and translocate the chemical to kill the roots of weeds and unwanted plants. If the border is to be replanted, dig out any remaining roots and follow this by cultivation and manuring in the early autumn (see p. 40). It

Above: Glyphosate has been applied to this neglected rock garden (see p.8)
Below: Ground elder is a persistent perennial weed that must be cleared completely before replanting can begin

may be desirable to introduce new top soil: the border will be better drained as a result and is usually more attractive if elevated a few inches above adjacent lawn or patio.

Also consider the possibility of changing the site of the old border, especially if it is positioned too near a privet or other hedge, whose roots, hungry for food and moisture, invade the area to the detriment of the border plants. A practical solution is often to resite the border a yard or so forward of its present position; or an island bed of oval or elliptical shape could be a pleasing alternative, sited as a focal point in clean ground which was formerly lawn (see p. 28). The old border area can then be cultivated and turfed or sown with grass seed, following application of herbicide or the digging out of weeds and unwanted plant growth. Three or four months of close mowing will prevent the survival of most of the remaining herbaceous plants, as well as ground elder and any other persistent perennial weeds.

ROCK GARDENS

A weed-infested rock garden is frequently a source of frustration, as perennial weeds, particularly buttercup, sorrel and bindweed (*Convolvulus*), become deeply entrenched beneath rocks, or tenaciously intertwined with any rock plant that has survived the period of neglect. Often, one or two rampant rock plants will have not only survived but tended to dominate and swamp more worthwhile but less vigorous neighbours. Particularly guilty in this respect are snow-in-summer (*Cerastium tomentosum*) and even the invasive shrubby ground cover, rose of Sharon (*Hypericum calycinum*). It is certainly best to dig out such plants if your aim is to restock with a fair range of interesting alpines. Glyphosate is again very useful for treating the entire area, after removing and reserving valued plants for the new planting. If there are bulbs present that you would like to keep, dig these out in clumps or wait until their foliage has died down before using the herbicide. If you are not happy with the quality of the rock or its arrangement, now is the opportunity to dismantle and rebuild, perhaps importing new rock and fresh top soil before replanting.

ROUGH AREAS AND ORCHARDS

Uncultivated parts of the garden can rapidly deteriorate into an impenetrable wilderness of scrambling and rampant perennial weeds. Bramble and nettle are universally troublesome and the beautiful but very invasive rosebay willowherb (*Epilobium angustifolium*) will often colonize burnt-over land where a bonfire has been. It can be daunting for a newcomer faced with this jungle-like situation. However, these weeds quickly succumb to the correct herbicide sensibly applied.

Bramble is best cut down to within a few inches of the ground and the top growth burnt; subsequent regrowth near ground level or from below can be effectively and conveniently treated with glyphosate or the individual plants dug out. Nettles can be similarly treated, ideally when regrowth is 6–9 in. (15–18 cm) high and growing vigorously. Rosebay willowherb seeds about prodigiously and will soon become a nuisance among other plants in cultivated borders, but it is shallow-rooted and easy to dig out if the area is not great. Glyphosate sprayed on young growth will clear up larger infestations, or dichlobenil can be applied successfully in February or March if the area is to remain uncultivated for at least another year.

On acid peaty soils, bracken (*Pteridium aquilinum*) is often prevalent and is difficult to treat chemically. On a small scale, digging out the rhizomes which are just below the surface is the most sensible course of action. Persistent hoeing of young growth from rhizomes missed in the digging-out exercise can rid the ground of bracken in one or two years. Regrettably, this method of control is not rewarding where creeping thistle (*Cirsium arvense*) is encountered, as fragments of the fleshy persistent roots are inevitably missed when attempting to dig out the weed. However, this troublesome thistle can be successfully controlled with glyphosate during the growing season, or by dichlobenil applied as recommended above for willowherb in fallow ground.

PROBLEM WEEDS

Horsetail (*Equisetum* species), Japanese knotweed (*Polygonum cuspidatum*), winter heliotrope (*Petasite fragrans*) and coltsfoot (*Tussilago farfara*) are probably the most serious of a short list of mainly vigorous, large-growing perennial weeds, which have deep persistent fleshy roots and which, once established, resist even the most efficient herbicides available today. If you have the misfortune to move to a garden where areas are infested with any of these weeds, you will find their eradication extremely difficult but not always impossible.

Where these problem weeds occur in uncultivated parts of the garden among mature or semi-mature trees and shrubs, it may be advisable to accept their presence in a limited patch; it is quite possible to keep them confined, to this by close-mowing an area of grass which butts up to it. If the growth of weed is not extensive, repeated digging out or hoeing will reduce the infestation or keep it within reasonable limits, allowing trees and other woody plants to grow without excessive competition. Chemical control can be partially successful, using dichlobenil granules applied in February or March when the soil is moist and before new spring growth emerges. However, this chemical may cause damage if the soil is dry and should not be used near herbaceous or bulbous plants, or woody plants established less than two years.

For problem weeds in cultivated areas, limited spot treatment may be possible during the growing season with glyphosate or amitrole plus MCPA. However, the best results will be achieved by temporarily removing any herbaceous plants and immature shrubs and fallowing the land for at least one growing season, allowing several weedkiller applications to take place before replanting. (See also *Wisley Handbook: Weed Control in the Garden*.)

Creeping thistle and horsetail are common perennial weeds, the latter is one of the most difficult plants to get rid of once established (see p. 9)

Large Trees

Several species of native trees are all too commonly found in our gardens, even in areas of fairly dense housing. Such large trees as ash (*Fraxinus excelsior*), horse chestnut (*Aesculus hippocastanum*) and sycamore (*Acer pseudoplatanus*) are quite unsuitable for small gardens, usually blocking light, invading building foundations and impoverishing growing space, as well as causing problems with their saplings or self-sown seedlings.

DEALING WITH UNSUITABLE TREES

After a period of neglect, dealing with undesirable trees or those that have grown excessively is often the most urgent task. Indeed, your plans for that greenhouse, rose garden, ornamental pool or other garden improvements will not make good sense unless it is possible at least to reduce the size and density of the crown of, say, a large sycamore which may be shading much of your garden from the south and west.

If the tree is in a neighbour's garden, there may be a case for its removal or pruning by mutual agreement. However, before you call in a tree surgeon, check with the arboricultural department of your local authority for possible Tree Preservation Orders (TPOs). You may reside in a conservation area which all tree felling is prohibited, though permission for qualified operators to carry out sensible or essential tree surgery is usually granted. Penalties for contravening these regulations are severe and fines of up to £2,000 are possible.

On the other hand, the law allows you to cut back overhanging growth of your neighbour's tree or shrub to the point of the boundary between you: if this is carried out too literally there can be a mass of ugly died-back branches or pruning stubs and the loss of shape or balance of a tree which may be important in the local scene. From the aesthetic viewpoint and with due regard to correct tree-surgery practice, branches or branchlets to be removed should be cut back to a convenient fork or nearly flush with the main trunk of the tree. Again, it pays to have a friendly relationship with your neighbour!

(For resiting of trees, see p. 20.)

TREATING SEEDLINGS AND SAPLINGS

Where sycamore, ash or horse chestnut are involved, the garden
will abound with their seedlings after a period of neglect. These can
rapidly make sizable saplings or small trees that are increasingly
difficult to deal with the longer they are left and are a particular
problem when immediately next to another valued tree or shrub, or
in the middle of a hedge, or hard against a wall or fence. Equally
troublesome in this respect are large shrubs or shrubby trees like
the native elder (*Sambucus nigra*) and goat willow (*Salix caprea*). If
you are not familiar with these natives, it is worth learning to
recognize them by summer foliage and winter twigs and dormant
buds, so that they can then be rooted out whenever the opportunity
occurs. All trees seedlings and saplings should be dug out
completely as quickly as possible, for even small saplings, if cut
down to near ground level, will usually regenerate to make vigorous
multi-stemmed bushes, eventually of some size. In uncultivated
areas, but only there, freshly cut stumps of larger saplings can be
successfully treated with ammonium sulphamate.

REMOVING STUMPS

I do most sincerely recommend that any dead, half-decayed or live
(often suckering) stumps of trees, whether felled by you or inherited
from earlier fellings, are completely removed as a priority. While
they remain, they occupy space which may be at a premium and, in
lawns, impede mowing. In addition, many common tree species –
ash, lime, elder, sycamore, willow – will seriously inhibit the
growth or establishment of new planting near by. Furthermore, dead
stumps harbour fungal diseases, most importantly honey fungus, as
the wood and roots rot in the ground.

Stumps and major roots should therefore be removed entirely
wherever possible. Excavation of larger stumps may be done by a
stump-chipping machine, nowadays hired or arranged through a
tree-surgery company and ranging from small hand-pushed to large
tractor-mounted models; to give access for the tractor, you may
have to remove a fence panel, or temporarily move a shrub or two
out of the way. Where there is adequate space to manoeuvre, a JCB
excavator will also take out stumps efficiently. If a larger tree is
available near by to act as an anchor, a simple hand-operated
'Tirfor' winch, usually obtainable from a local plant-hire company,
is a most useful tool for extracting trees, large shrubs and stumps
without need for bulky machinery. Failing all these methods, one

A stump-chipping machine can be hired to reduce tree stumps to sawdust. Protective clothing should be worn when using such equipment

usually has to resort to hand-digging, which is perhaps the best way for the odd small stump. I am reluctant to recommend chemicals to dispose of stumps, other than in unimportant corners of the garden. The use of ammonium sulphamate or potassium (or sodium) nitrate, followed by burning, can be successful, but is inevitably a slow process and may tend to poison the ground locally.

HONEY FUNGUS AND OTHER DISEASES

The most important and dreaded disease associated with tree stumps – **honey fungus** (*Armillaria* species) is all too common. This disease may have caused the death of the tree, leaving white fungal strands and sometimes black rhizomorphs (bootlace-like structures) usually under the bark of the stump and among the roots to grow out and infect healthy trees and shrubs in a slowly widening area. Apart from removing stumps, approved chemical means are now available to *treat* honey fungus where it occurs in gardens and even, it is claimed, to cure certain infected shrubs and small trees. Phenolic emulsion can be applied to the collar of an infected woody

A tree stump with honey fungus should be removed to prevent the spread of this disease. Toadstools are not always produced

plant, in an effort to save it. The same emulsion is recommended as a sterilant, to prevent the spread of the disease from an infected area.

If trees, shrubs or hedge plants have died and the presence of honey fungus is suspected, do seek expert advice (see also p. 64).

There are several other all too prevalent diseases that one should look out for in a neglected garden. **Coral spot** (*Nectria cinnabarina*) is very common, appearing as bright pink or red pustules on dead branches of a wide range of trees and shrubs. From the dead, it frequently invades live tissue, causing die-back or wilt. Good garden hygiene is the best way to control this disease: remove and burn dead wood left from pruning; never leave dead pruning stubs; and treat major cuts with a wound sealant containing a fungicide.

Fireblight (*Erwinia amylovora*), although no longer a notifiable disease of fruit trees, is now widespread and found as well on many ornamental shrubs of the rose family (Rosaceae) particularly *Cotoneaster*, hawthorn (*Crataegus*), *Pyracantha*, rowan (*Sorbus*) and *Stranvaesia*. This troublesome bacterial disease attacks both growing and flowering shoots, causing die-back and giving the appearance that the plant has been scorched by fire. If the shrub or tree is heavily infected, it is best to uproot and burn it; limited infection can be cut back until no brown stain is evident in the wood. Wounds should be sealed and the shrub or tree fed with a compound

14

Pink pustules denote the presence of coral spot. All infected wood should be cut out and burned immediately

fertilizer such as Growmore or Vitax Q4, to induce good growth. All prunings must be burnt and pruning tools and knives disinfected with a 3 per cent lysol solution.

Phytophthora root death (*Phytophthora* species) is a fungal disease which kills roots. It is responsible for the death of a wide range of ornamental trees and shrubs, including fruit trees and particularly conifers. The disease is difficult to diagnose accurately, especially if the plant has been dead for some time, when the primary cause of death is often masked by a secondary infection of honey fungus. The disease is favoured by moist warm soils and excessive use of farmyard manure and organic mulches. Although until recently phytophthora was common throughout the tree and shrub nursery trade, container-growing has much reduced its incidence. In gardens, infected plants must be rooted out and burnt with the minimum of delay and the site sterilized before back-filling with clean soil (for further advice, see p. 64).

Shrubs and Small Trees

After very few years of neglect and lack of pruning, especially if too closely planted initially, many shrubs will have grown into a congested mass, devoid of shape and form and usually suppressing one another. This situation can often be improved by removing over-vigorous or unsuitable shrubs, while pruning others to create more shapely, compact specimens, and by resiting smaller ones.

RENOVATING OVERGROWN SHRUBS AND SMALL TREES

During the winter months is a good time to set about the renovation of any overgrown hardy shrubs that you have decided to retain as part of the new garden scheme. They often form an important part of the garden architecture and can provide useful instant maturity when reconstructing a neglected garden. Familiar shrubs which respond to severe stooling include the many worthwhile cultivars of

Gold-splashed *Elaeagnus pungens* 'Maculata' is being overwhelmed by the grey-green sucker growth of the more vigorous rootstock

common lilac (*Syringa vulgaris*). These may have grown leggy and misshapen, reaching tree-like proportions with trunks 3–4 in. (8–10 cm) in diameter. In such a case, reduce the leggy specimen with a saw until you have a compact framework of short, well spaced limbs, say 3–6 ft (1–2 m) in overall height. In spring, new growth will emerge from the bare wood and can be selectively thinned to form a neat, well balanced shrub. This often proves a very rewarding exercise, even though loss of flower for two or three years is inevitable. Tall and leggy Hardy Hybrid rhododendrons and deciduous azaleas can be similarly treated – as indeed can many other hardy, mainly evergreen shrubs which tend to develop tree-like growth as they mature and have the capacity to respond to hard pruning by producing vigorous growth from old wood. Among these we can include our native evergreens holly (*Ilex*), yew (*Taxus*) and box (*Buxus*) and, in addition, *Elaeagnus*, *Euonymus*, *Olearia*, *Osmanthus* (*Osmarea*), *Phillyrea*, *Photinia*, *Pyracantha* and *Viburnum*.

Sucker growth or 'volunteer' rootstock is a frequent problem, particularly with old grafted plants of lilac, rhododendron, *Elaeagnus* and *Viburnum*. Regrettably, severe cutting back of the shrub has the disadvantage of encouraging rootstock growth; with *Elaeagnus* and *Viburnum* the foliage of the rootstock is usually distinct, but the leaves of *Rhododendron ponticum* bear close resemblance to those of many Hardy Hybrids for which it is used as a rootstock and careful comparison in necessary. If allowed to persist, these sucker growths, which are always more vigorous, will rapidly depress the desired shrub grafted on them. I find evidence of this in almost every neglected garden I visit. No time should be lost in identifying and removing sucker growths, carefully digging below ground where necessary and keeping a constant watch for any recurring shoots. It is not sufficient to cut off suckers at ground level, as they will quickly regenerate and continue to sap the energy of the plant. Most garden trees which have been produced by budding or grafting will tend to suffer from the same complaint and again urgent action is needed. Volunteer sucker growth is especially common with cherries (*Prunus*), ornamental crabs (*Malus*), thorns (*Crataegus*) and mountain ash and whitebeam (*Sorbus*).

Other essential pruning will involve mainly deciduous shrubs which have suffered neglect and become a forest of congested stems, both thin and weak and thick and exhausted. Familiar shrubs which fall into this category include *Deutzia*, *Kolkwitzia*, *Philadelphus* and *Weigela*. These produce flowers on the previous season's growth and healthy vigorous specimens are normally thinned and pruned annually after flowering. However, with old congested bushes, it is often best to start again by reducing all growth to near ground level and selectively thinning new shoots to form a well spaced and balanced branch system; there will be no flowers for two or three years. After renovation, feeding with Growmore or, better still, a slow-release compound fertilizer is essential to achieve the best results. Mulching with well rotted farmyard manure or pulverized bark will also greatly assist the speedy recovery of the shrubs, together with attention to watering in times of drought.

In some cases, where the shrub is not only overgrown and exhausted, but may be a cultivar with little floral impact and now superseded, it is wiser to dig out the old giant – perhaps using a JCB excavator which has been hired to deal with tree stumps. A vigorous young specimen of a worthwhile cultivar can be planted as a replacement after generous preparation of the site. (See p. 40.)

Mature but healthy plants of Old-fashioned, Bourbon, Hybrid Musk and other shrub roses will also respond to quite severe pruning and thinning of congested growth. These, if rightly sited, can be important in the structure of the renovated garden. After some years of neglect, suckers of briar rootstock, showing distinct foliage and habit, may have grown prodigiously and will need careful removal from below ground where they join the parent plant, in the same way as with other budded or grafted shrubs.

I am a great believer in the value of feeding shrubs which have been renovated in this way; equally, shrub roses will respond to generous applications of rose fertilizer or one of the slow-release compounds (Vitax Q4 or Enmag).

RESTORING AND SUPPORTING CLIMBERS AND WALL SHRUBS

Within only two or three years of planting, the more vigorous climbing roses, honeysuckle (*Lonicera*), clematis and wisteria, as well as popular wall shrubs like evergreen *Ceanothus* and *Pyracantha*, all require annual pruning, training and support. If not attended to, these plants will quickly outgrow their allotted space on walls, fences and pergolas and become tangled and confused.

Above: Climbers such as clematis can soon get out of control unless pruned regularly and new growth trained in

Below: Hydrid Musk roses such as 'Cornelia' will respond well to feeding after a period of neglect

On a neglected property, the original support, if provided, may also have rotted or rusted away and often a variety of unsuitable nails may have been used ineffectively.

It is well worth assessing the condition of the support and arranging to replace it, if necessary, before or shortly after installing new climbers and wall shrubs, or in conjunction with pruning, renovating and restarting existing plants. Ideally, galvanized or white metal vine eyes 3–4 in. (8–10 cm) long and of the screw-in type should be used. These are inserted in walls, with a Rawlplug, into neatly drilled holes spaced about 3 ft (1 m) apart, in ranks 1 ft (30 cm) apart, or are screwed directly into wooden fence posts. Aluminium, galvanized or green plastic-covered wire, which is reasonably long-lasting, should then be stretched as tautly as possible between the vine eyes. Alternatively, trellis can be used. Garden twine or purpose-made plastic ties are used to secure the climber or wall shrubs to the wire or trellis.

RESITING SHRUBS AND TREES

You may inherit some shrubs that have been established a few years and were initially too closely planted. Resiting to allow for ultimate growth is usually possible, particularly if the shrub has a shallow fibrous root system and is in good health. *Pieris* and hydrangeas come into this category, while rhododendrons and azaleas, with their pads of fine fibrous roots, will move at almost any size. Late winter or early spring is the best time to transplant a shrub, taking care to lift the plant with a generous root ball of moist soil. Having selected the new site with due regard for eventual growth of the shrub, thoroughly prepare the soil. Ensure that the transplant is well firmed in and, if necessary, securely staked and that watering and mulching are carried out in the spring and summer of the following two years. Here is the opportunity to prune and shape the shrub as it is moved; many evergreens can be helped to recover by cutting back top growth by up to 50 per cent, thereby substantially reducing the leaf area through which the shrub will lose moisture by transpiration.

If you are attempting to resite an established tree (or shrub) of semi-mature size, say 10 ft (3 m) or more in height, its chances of successful re-establishment can be greatly improved by preparing it for the move. During winter or early spring, trench around and partly undermine the plant, cleanly cutting roots up to 1 in. (3 cm) in diameter, to encourage the formation of a fibrous root ball of convenient size – usually not less than 2 ft (60 cm) in diameter. Then

Preparation to resite an established tree should be carried out before the growing season gets underway, at least a year in advance of moving

back-fill the trench with a peat and sand/soil mixture and a handful of bonemeal or slow-release fertilizer. During the following growing season, when water should be given in any drought periods, new fibrous roots will form. The tree or shrub can be moved to its new site during the next lifting season, but no later than early March for deciduous trees and shrubs and April for evergreens. Some careful thinning or reduction of the crown may help to prevent partial or even total die-back of twigs or branches.

With semi-mature plants, it is vital to ensure that watering, mulching, shading and sheltering are not neglected, particularly in exposed sites. A smaller specimen will benefit if sheltered and shaded by cut branches, renewed as needed, of cypress or another evergreen stuck in the ground around the transplant; alternatively use green plastic mesh windbreak, obtainable in various sizes from garden centres. A larger deciduous tree, with a trunk 3 in. (10 cm) or more in width, will be assisted in re-establishment if the trunk and major branches are bound with hessian or plastic tape, particularly in exposed sunny positions. Do not forget that your resited large shrub or tree will require efficient staking or securing (see pp. 43–4). Finally, if you are resiting a specimen tree or shrub in rough-cut grass or close-mown lawn, give it at least a 3–5 ft (1–1.5 m) diameter circle of soil; this should be mulched with bark to conserve moisture and to reduce invasion by grass and weeds, which will compete for food and moisture with the transplant struggling to re-establish.

Hedges

REDUCING OVERGROWN HEDGES

It is usually important to maintain effective dense boundary hedges to keep out animals as well as people. Most hedges plants are so used because they respond by forming thick, virtually impenetrable growth. Thorn, field maple, beech and the evergreens holly, yew, laurel (common and Portugal) and cypress (Lawson and Leyland) are all frequently chosen. With neglect, they can become unnecessarily tall and wide, often with holes at the base allowing entry of the neighbour's dog. However, with the exception of beech and Leyland cypress which have grown without restriction to about 16 ft (5 m) or more, most neglected hedges can be reduced to more manageable dimensions of 5–8 ft (1.5–2.5 m) high and 1½–2½ ft (0.5–0.8 m) wide.

The work of renovation is best carried out during winter or early spring, using a saw, heavy clippers and secateurs to cut to a point a few inches below the desired future height. Excessive width should be dealt with by cutting back one side of the hedge almost to the main stem one year and repeating the process on the other side a year later. Combined with generous feeding, mulching with farmyard manure and watering, this rather drastic treatment is quite successful. Furthermore, the hedge remains as a barrier and screen while its renovation proceeds, which is not so if the hedge is reduced to near ground level, as is sometimes advised.

Neglected hedges within the garden – frequently box (*Buxus*), yew (*Taxus*), *Berberis*, *Escallonia*, *Lonicera nitida* or *Viburnum tinus* – will respond to similar treatment, preferably in spring when new growth is commencing.

REINFORCING THIN HEDGES

Although perhaps the best course of action, it is not always practical to root out a poor thin hedge and start again. This accepted, it is usually possible to improve density and fill basal gaps with transplants of the same species. However, owing to competition with existing hedge plants for root space, as well as food and moisture, progress is often slow and the casualty rate of transplants high.

Sycamore, elder and brambles need careful grubbing from this neglected holly hedge; bindweed is best treated with glyphosate in early summer

Another method of filling gaps is to plant dense compact evergreens about 3 ft (1 m) clear of the hedge line. A temporary screen of wire netting or plastic mesh may be needed to cover low holes in the hedge if the neighbour's dog is a problem. A barrier of slates, tiles or heavy-duty polythene, inserted in the soil on the hedge side of the new shrubs, is advantageous to prevent vigorous feeding roots of the hedge from invading their root space. Neat, clippable, and, if need be, spiny shrubs suitable for this task can help to transform a tatty hedge into a feature of beauty.

As an extension of this idea, a poor thin (usually deciduous) boundary hedge can be effectively reinforced (if replacement is impracticable) with reliable taller hardy evergreens. Planted on the inside well clear of the hedge line, in an informal arrangement about 4–5 ft (1.2–1.5 m) apart, these will blend together to give colour and interest of flower, foliage and berry throughout the year (see p.46ff. for suggestions). As a result, you will have an adequate evergreen screen without the need to clip a formal hedge and a good background for other planting or features within the garden.

Equally, a collection of evergreens can be used to screen a new, rather stark interwoven panel or closeboard fence or an ugly wall. Plant ideally about 3 ft (1 m) from the fence to allow room for growth and space for maintenance of the fence when required.

Roses

In deference to our national flower, even the smallest garden will boast a few rose bushes. So often, however, attempts are made to grow bedding roses – Hybrid Tea and Floribunda (now correctly known as Large flowered and Cluster flowered respectively) – on the most impoverished and unsuitable soils. Bedding roses are gross feeders which grow and flower best on rich loams and clays; they will require heavy feeding and manuring to give anything approaching an acceptable performance on poor soils, whether sandy, gravelly, chalky or peaty. After a period of neglect, bedding roses on these soils will have greatly deteriorated through disease and lack of feeding. Even on more suitable soils, where beds have carried roses for many years, deterioration is inevitable without regular feeding and mulching and spraying against disease. An additional problem, with neglect, is that the soil tends to become 'rose-sick', usually making a resoiling and manuring exercise necessary if bedding roses are to be grown again to a reasonable standard in the same beds.

Rose-sick soil and sucker growth make this rose bed a sorry sight; so grub up the bushes, improve the soil and plant something different (see pp. 61–3)

ROSE-SICKNESS

Assuming the planting of roses on the site is desired and remains appropriate, remove all dead or deteriorating rose bushes, then dig out at least the top 6 in. (15 cm) of soil, which will be heavily infested with disease spores, and remove from the site. Following a generous application of manure dug into the excavated area, backfill with fresh, top-spit, loamy soil, preferably from stacked turves; this is essential if bedding roses are to be anything approaching well grown in districts where the natural soil is poor. Allow several weeks for settlement before planting.

In the case of a larger rose garden with ideal soil, where a rose-sick condition has developed over some years but a soil change is both awkward and very expensive, professional soil sterilization is a possible solution, using dazomet, formaldehyde or a related fumigant. Seek further detailed advice from your local branch of ADAS (Agricultural Development and Advisory Service), whose address should be available from the local public library.

CONVERTING ROSE BEDS

Apart from impoverished or rose-sick soils, I sometimes find that trees have grown up over the years in the vicinity of a rose garden, casting heavy shade over the roses and invading the soil with their roots. Occasionally, there may be the added complication of a Tree Preservation Order on the tree or trees involved, or the fact that the owner does not wish them removed. Obviously, the beds are no longer suitable for bedding roses, which require both sunshine and rich soil. In such circumstances, an acceptable solution may be to convert the planting to shrubs, using a variety of predominantly evergreen and shade-tolerant dwarf shrubs, with potential as flowering, berrying or foliage plants.

Low-growing herbaceous plants can also be included in careful association with the shrubs. If the beds of the rose garden are in a formal arrangement, a diagonally matching planting will look well at all seasons, although there will not be the impact of colour possible from roses (see plans on pp. 61–2).

Lawns

Although a lawn might seem the first and most obvious area needing attention in a neglected garden, it is sensible to leave it until heavy work, especially where machines are involved, and major replanting have been completed.

RENEWING A NEGLECTED LAWN

Take a critical look at your neglected lawn. If it is bumpy and unpleasant to walk on, it has probably been mown erratically or not at all for a year or more. In such circumstances, it is very likely that coarse broad-leaved grasses will have taken over, suppressing the finer lawn grasses. To achieve a lawn of reasonable quality, it would be better to consider remaking the lawn in spring or autumn by seeding or turfing. This would ensure a lawn of good appearance and easy maintenance.

However, closer examination may show that fine lawn grasses still predominate, with small patches of coarse grasses perhaps widely spaced but beginning to spread; there may also be a fair sprinkling of broad-leaved lawn weeds – creeping buttercup, daisy, dandelion, yarrow and clover. In this case, renovation is possible and usually successful.

It is advisable to start work in the spring, using a rotary or hover-type mowing machine if necessary and reducing the height of the long grass progressively over two or three weeks, until a height of about ¾ in. (2 cm) is reached. Now is the time to apply a lawn fertilizer appropriate to the season; watering should also be carried out if there is a spring drought. At this stage, hand-weeding of patches of coarse grasses should be tackled: regrettably, there are no chemical means of dealing selectively with coarse grasses as there are for the majority of broad-leaved lawn weeds. The latter, including the more resistant yarrow and clover, can be treated during late spring and summer with one or two applications of a lawn weedkiller based on 2,4-D, usually combined with dicamba or mecaprop. An extra boost is given to fine lawn grasses if a liquid fertilizer rich in nitrogen is applied shortly before or combined with the selective weedkiller. This will encourage grasses to recolonize small bare patches where weeds have died or coarse grasses have

Left: Moss and algae can be a problem where a lawn is badly drained. They can take over unless measures are taken to improve the situation
Right: Glyphosate can be used to kill grass where a new bed is needed or to mark the site where a specimen tree is to be planted

been weeded out. Larger patches may need local cultivation plus a little fresh top soil and a pinch or two of lawn grass seed. Unless the lawn can be frequently irrigated and kept moist, it is best not to apply weedkillers or fertilizers in periods of drought.

During the summer months and into the autumn, begin a regime of regular mowing. Periodic rolling is invariably necessary, as neglected lawns tend to become uneven with the action of frost, and should be carried out when the ground is moist and therefore pliable. Annual rolling may well be required each spring in the future; if you have not inherited a suitable roller with the garden, it may be worth purchasing one unless hiring facilities exist locally.

MOSS ON LAWNS

Moss is a problem often giving cause for great concern. Our moist autumn and winter months favour its growth, notably in badly drained conditions and in shaded gardens overhung with trees. Improvement of the drainage may help but, in heavily shaded areas, lawns can deteriorate to the point where little grass is left and moss has taken over. If this is not acceptable, it is worth planting attractive and permanent ground cover, which is more likely to succeed in these conditions than grass (see pp. 51–6 for recommended plants).

In some gardens, moss itself is encouraged to make a green carpet; indeed, it arrives naturally in shaded areas after repeated applications of paraquat or glyphosate to control weeds between shrubs. Stepping stones of natural stone or oak discs from a felled tree can provide access. At the Savill Garden, Windsor Great Park, there is a famous example of a moss garden, where an expanse of white forked moss (*Leucobryum glaucum*) makes a much admired feature under large beech trees.

All this said, you may wish to retain your conventional lawn if at all possible. Where a good proportion of fine grasses remains amid the moss and the lawn area is not overhung with large forest trees growing larger each year, then a spring treatment with a proprietary moss-killer, preferably combined with fertilizer, is usually effective. However, when drainage is at fault, an attempt must be made to investigate and cure the problem – perhaps by hollow-tining followed by top-dressing, or even by mole- or pipe-draining. In our climate and in spite of our best efforts, the moss tends to return in the cool moist conditions of autumn, although if all these measures are taken, a dense sward of vigorous lawn grasses should reduce the chance of moss recolonizing.

CONVERTING GRASS TO FLOWER BEDS

Sometimes, you may wish to extend an existing flower bed or border into the lawn. First, carefully mark out the area involved. Unless the turf is required elsewhere in the garden, in which case it should be removed carefully, apply glyphosate with a sprayer or fine-rose watering can. Then leave for 10 to 14 days in summer and three to four weeks in winter before spreading manure or compost and rotovating or hand-digging. This herbicide will kill the grass without leaving any toxic residue; the dead grass and root fibre will add humus to the soil, but will not regenerate to be a weed nuisance in the cultivated ground.

Structural Repairs

Early attention should be given to the repair or replacement of fences and garden wall, paths and paved areas, and ornamental pools. However, work involving the use of cement or concrete is best avoided in the winter months.

FENCES

Fence posts often rot at or about ground level and, if they are of good oak or other hardwood, they may be sound, though aged, above this. Today, metal or concrete base posts or 'grandfathers' are obtainable to which the sound fence tops can be bolted. Where wooden fences have rotted and need replacement, consider the use of chain-link fencing. Unobtrusive green PVC covering a strong galvanized core makes a sturdy inexpensive barrier, up to 6 ft (2 m) high; it is very suitable for use in conjunction with resited semi-mature shrubs (see p. 20) when some immediate screening is necessary.

BOUNDARY WALLS

Walls can be made of a range of materials, from concrete blocks to mellow brick, or a mixture of flints, natural stone, brick and even chalk boulders. Such mixtures weather at different rates and, with time, will fall into disrepair. When rebuilding, I certainly favour recycling existing hard materials (other than concrete) wherever possible; the soft lime mortar used long ago to cement old garden walls should be easy to clean from old bricks, flints and stones before these are reused.

DRY-STONE WALLS

Walls retaining soil banks may eventually crumble. It is invariably better to reconstruct them, reusing natural durable stone like Purbeck or Cotswold limestone if it is still in good condition and adding further matching pieces as necessary. Roughly rectangular pieces not less than 2 in. (5 cm) thick should be used; or a variety of thicknesses – even chunky pieces up to 6 in. (15 cm) thick – can achieve a pleasing effect. Be sure to build with a 'batter' so that the

A retaining drystone wall built at an angle and planted with valerian (*Centranthus ruber*) and *Erigeron mucronatus* (*E. karvinskianus*)

face of the wall is set back 20° from the vertical to prevent future subsidence.

If plants were used in the original wall, some of those with good fibrous roots can be replanted, sandwiching the spread-out roots between layers of soil 1–2 in. (3–5 cm) thick, which should form the 'mortar' between the stones. Moist, fibrous, loamy soil from stacked turf is ideal for this work, which is best carried out between autumn and early spring when conditions are likely to remain consistently cool and damp, enabling the 'soil-mortar' to settle and the plants to re-establish. At this time of year also, new pot-grown plants can be successfully installed in the wall as construction proceeds, spacing them not less than 2 ft (60 cm) apart in a staggered arrangement, at stone junctions or in vertical crevices. There are many good alpine plants for year-round effect to drape a dry-stone wall and they are often spectacular in flower (see p.57). A selection of these plants, once established will prevent soil erosion and help to bind the wall.

PAVED AREAS

Similarly, terraces, patios and steps paved with natural stone can be refurbished where frost has shattered the surface after several

One way to improve the look of damaged paving is to plant between the cracks with low, spreading subjects such as heathers and thymes

winters of neglect and made walking hazardous. Turn over or replace the defective stones, carefully rebedding them on sand. A period of neglect usually results in an invasion of troublesome perennial weeds: dandelion, dock and ground elder are the chief culprits. A heavy long-established infestation may necessitate lifting the stones and thoroughly clearing weed roots before relaying. Alternatively, a translocating herbicide containing amitrole or glyphosate can be used effectively, but will delay any proposed planting.

Following weed-killing, repair or relaying, the addition of suitable paving plants will do much to enhance a renovated patio. Many have scented flowers or foliage (see pp. 57–8). It may be necessary to lift stones and prepare the ground beneath, particularly if there is concrete or hardcore present which may need to be removed, although broader gaps between stones or chipped-off corners often give enough space for planting. Any old planting sites should be resoiled with John Innes compost No. 1 or 2. Natural stone paving, whether crazy or random rectangular, is best if you wish to add plants to a paved area. Space the plants irregularly at least 3 ft (1 m) apart to allow for growth and do not forget to leave adequate access for walking, although some plants will tolerate a certain amount of trampling.

ORNAMENTAL POOLS

Pools make a charming feature, but they can also present problems; indeed, a leaking concrete, plastic or fibreglass garden pool, densely congested with rampant water plants, is a familiar sight in many neglected gardens.

First, decide if the pond is sensibly sited, that is, in an open situation well clear of deciduous trees, which would shade it and fill it with autumn leaves. If it is and renovation is worthwhile, completely clean out the pool in early spring, saving a small amount of any plants which you intend to replant and temporarily accommodating them in a container of shallow water. Unfortunately, many of popular aquatic plants, such as the water or flag iris (*Iris pseudoacorus*) and reed-mace (*Typha latifolia*, often wrongly called bulrush), are much too rampant for small garden pools, as

An overgrown pool in want of clearing. It is choked with yellow nuphar and blue pickerel weed (*Pontederia cordata*)

are some of the more vigorous water lilies (*Nymphaea*). It is usually better to replace these with smaller-growing more compact marginal plants or water lily cultivars (see p. 58).

Repair kits are available to deal with cracks or tears in fibreglass and PVC pools and attempts can be made to repair leaks and cracks in poorly constructed concrete ponds with bitumastic paint or filler. However, since the damage to a concrete pool is usually due to frost, which is likely to recur, a butyl rubber liner (laid on a fibreglass blanket) over the concrete will provide a more reliable long-term repair. To calculate the size of liner, add twice the greatest depth of the pool to both the length and the breadth and multiply the two sums to obtain the square measurement needed.

Replant in May or June, using purpose-made plastic planting crates, obtainable from water plant specialists, to restrict marginal plants and water lilies. These crates taper sharply to the bottom and, on sloping surfaces or in an exposed situation should be surrounded with bricks or stone to prevent them from falling on their sides. Use heavy loamy soil for aquatics and water lilies and surface the crates with small pebbles. The butyl liner may be covered effectively with larger pebbles. Remember to include submerged oxygenating plants (for example, *Elodea crispa* and *Callitriche verna*) to help maintain a good balance of wild life and to discourage the formation of algae, which is responsible for green water and blanket weed. With water lilies, elevate the crates on bricks so that they are positioned initially no more than 4–5 in. (12–15 cm) below the surface and any formed leaves are not submerged; then lower the plants to the pool floor as the leaves extend. Place them well away from cascades and fountains, as they do not relish the continual play of water on leaves and flowers. Finally, do not introduce fish until plant life is growing vigorously – usually a month or more after planting.

Redesigning

By now, you will have decided what main features you would like to see in your refurbished garden. Do ensure that these are both advisable and practical. For instance, if you would like a greenhouse or conservatory to grow sun-loving plants or crops, can it be suitably sited in an unshaded area and remain aesthetically acceptable within the garden scene? Will the position you have in mind for a new garden pool, rose garden or herb garden be open to sunshine and free from tall overhanging trees now and in the future? Is the soil suitable for the rhododendrons and other acid-loving shrubs that you were considering for a shady situation? (If in doubt, soil-testing kits are available from your local garden centre.) These are some of the basic questions that you should be asking as you set about the task of reconstituting the neglected garden.

PLANS OR MARKING OF SITES

As with new unplanted plots, mature gardens which have been largely cleared of unwanted trees and shrubs lend themselves to what one might call 'drawing-board planning'; this is essential where a design involving hard surfaces is required and a reasonably accurate survey, often combined with taking of levels, will be necessary.

However, I have already mentioned how desirable it is to retain or resite the worthiest of existing shrubs and smaller trees, to form the bones of the new scheme. Accurate surveying and positioning of these on a drawing can be a complicated and time-consuming business and, apart from small focal-point plantings, is usually best avoided. Instead, I adopt a system of marking positions for new or resited trees, shrubs, roses and ground-cover plants, using bamboo canes and hanging plastic or manilla labels, on which the names are written in pencil (2B) or waterproof ink (if there is likely to be a delay of several months before planting takes place). This method is both accurate and inexpensive, but it is still worth making a rough sketch of the arrangement as the labels can be blown away in gales, particularly in an exposed garden, while small children or the family's dog may collect or even rearrange the marking canes! Carry out any transplanting as soon as possible in the dormant season (see p.20). New planting can then follow in prepared ground in planned relationship to the maturing specimens.

For important focal-point plantings, small plans on paper are certainly worth the time spent: indeed if the area is empty or nearly so any surveying will be minimal. (See pp. 59–60) for plans for north- and south-facing aspects.)

PRACTICAL CONSIDERATIONS

It is important to allow for a compost heap in the new scheme; it needs to be readily accessible for depositing vegetable waste from house and garden as well as lawn mowings. A corner at one end of the garden is often appropriate, with an access path winding through a shrub border, in which evergreens can be carefully sited to afford screening at all seasons. If you have room for a bonfire or incinerator, this will also require screening and should be positioned away from the house and sitting-out areas and clear of overhanging trees or shrubs, which might catch fire or be damaged by heat.

Uninterrupted access around the house is invariably essential, especially where windows are involved. This usually means a paved or gravel path. Much frequented routes and short cuts – for example, from garage to back or front entrance – need to be hard-surfaced and open at all times; these paths tend to be made if they do not already exist, often to the detriment of lawn or border. Avoid planting thorny shrubs or roses near by which, in a year or two, are likely to catch in clothing as you pass.

PRIVACY AND SCREENING

Privacy is valuable, especially in built-up areas, and we resent incursion upon it. Equally most of us dislike having unsightly objects continually within view, whether garden sheds, greenhouses, neighbouring houses (particularly those with windows overlooking your garden or patio), telegraph poles festooned with wire, electrical transformer equipment and not-so-distant pylons or factory chimneys. To screen these, dense evergreen conifers are recommended, notably Lawson cypress cultivars like *Chamaecyparis lawsoniana* 'Fletcheri' (grey), 'Pembury Blue' and 'Stardust' (golden). Although slower in growth than the ubiquitous and ultimately over-large Leyland cypress, they are more compact and controllable by trimming with a long-arm pruner; I suggest it is worth waiting slightly longer, as any of these beautiful cypresses will hide an ugly installation and provide a focal point of colour and interest at all times of year. Take care to avoid planting in positions where growth will conflict with overhead wires.

Interwoven panel or closeboard fencing is very commonly used to give immediate privacy and to divide gardens into rigid rectangles; personally, I feel that these often necessary barriers are among the most hideous objects possible in the garden. Screening the fence with plant life makes it much more attractive. Even better is to aim for its eventual replacement with a variety of prunable hardy evergreens, which can also provide an excellent background for other planting within the garden (see p. 46 ff.). If the fence has to be accepted indefinitely, a trellis-top will give support for climbers such as clematis, honeysuckle and climbing roses, some of which will effectively spill down over the shrubs and give an extended floral display.

DIVIDING A LARGE GARDEN

It is a common situation today for a large property to be divided into flats or wings, each with its own separate part of the garden. Although an 'open-plan' arrangement, involving as much as possible of the old garden, is the most satisfactory, residents will understandably insist on a private area for their personal use. Existing permanent features like yew and box hedges should be preserved if at all feasible and these can even be moved, as they have fibrous roots (see p. 20). Further planting of suitable screening evergreens (see p. 46 ff.) may be necessary, in association with existing shrubs or hedges, to form a basis for these secluded gardens. Here is the opportunity to avoid ugly and expensive new fencing, except perhaps wattle hurdles as a temporary screen while new plants are making growth. It is a good ideas to come to an agreement over sharing the use of such facilities as the vegetable garden and fruit cage, which may be long established in the most appropriate sites in the old garden.

The dividing of a larger property may be more complicated when new houses are to be built in the garden; this often causes the destruction of old productive fruit trees. While the loss of these may have to be accepted, efforts should be made to conserve any particularly valued or known rare plants, by taking cuttings or

Above: A border of shade-loving, ground cover plants, including hostas and hardy geraniums, requires surprisingly little maintenance once established
Below: A low-maintenance feature can be created out of a combination of hard materials. Plant with shrubs and bulbs, and the area can be enjoyed throughout the year

scions for grafting, ideally during winter while dormant. Your county branch of NCCPG should be able to help (see p.64). Existing trees and shrubs deserve to be kept wherever possible. Specimens of up to semi-mature size, which conflict with the new development, can often be successfully resited before ground is levelled for the new building. While the autumn and winter months are ideal for this operation (see p. 20), it is certainly worth the effort of moving an otherwise doomed but valuable plant at other seasons, even during the summer and without advance preparation. Copious watering a day or two before the move is essential in this case and help may be obtainable from the contractors, who can play their part in conservation by lifting that much loved camellia or rhododendron, transporting it across the garden and digging a hole for it with a JCB excavator, before levelling the site of the new house.

LOW-MAINTENANCE FEATURES

These days, most people are anxious to have a labour-saving but attractive garden. Small areas of lawn help to set off other features and provide sitting-out places, but large expanses, particularly in small gardens, can be overwhelming and uninteresting, as well as labour-intensive in terms of weekly mowing from April to October, not to mention applying fertilizer and controlling weeds.

Ground-cover plants enable many gardeners to reach a compromise over some of the areas formerly devoted to lawn or rough-cut grass. Well chosen, permanent plantings, once established, require only the minimum of maintenance – usually tidying and dead-heading and perhaps a spring application of fertilizer. In return, they provide year-round textural interest, with colour from flower, foliage and berry. The range of plants, both shrubby and herbaceous, now commercially available is large, some might say bewildering. However, they can be grouped according to whether they are sun-loving or shade-tolerant, slow-growing and compact, or of average vigour, or fast-growing (but not rampant, for these are best grown on their own). By selecting within these groups (see p. 51–6), one can hopefully ensure that no plant will swamp its neighbour. Much of the art of gardening lies in associating plants according to colour, shape and texture of foliage and flower. Beyond the obvious practical considerations of sun or shade and degree of vigour, it is largely a question of taste and artistic sense, combined with an element of trial and error. Most plants are obliging and you can move them around the next season if you feel another position is to be preferred.

Bricks form a neat edging to a raised area of grass planted with soft grey *Ballota*, silvery *Helichrysum* and *Lonicera nitida* 'Baggesen's Gold'

When considering quantities to purchase or propagate, think in terms of three to five herbaceous or shrubby permanent ground-cover plants of each chosen variety to furnish an irregular patch roughly 3 ft (1 m) in diameter. Resist the temptation to indulge in too many sorts within a small area or the result can be fussy; usually no more than three different species or cultivars of similar vigour and rate of spread to 54sq.ft (5 m²) is about right in a small garden. Height and further interest can be provided by the addition of widely spaced, small specimen shrubs (see p. 50–1).

Gravel, pebbles and paving in recent years, visitors to Chelsea Flower Show have admired many well designed small gardens demonstrating the use of paving and pebble or gravel in place of grass or lawn; this labour-saving form of garden design is enjoying increasing popularity.

Gravel, shingle or pebble, ideally rounded or water-worn, can be had in a range of sizes, from pea-gravel to large Chesil beach pebble. A subtle mixture is often used as the main constituent of the design, perhaps blended with stepping stones of natural stone (York, Purbeck, Forest of Dean etc.), or brick paviors or sets, or patterned or riven-surfaced precast paving in various pastel shades. A well arranged combination of pebble and paving, associated with a satisfying array of shrubs and other plants, together giving colour, shape and varying textures at all seasons, is surely one of the most labour-saving and artistically acceptable of all garden arrangements.

Preparing the Ground and Replanting

In previous chapters, I have discussed the earliest priorities when endeavouring to reclaim a neglected garden – tree surgery, dealing with stumps, pruning and resiting shrubs, coping with perennial weeds and so on. You will also have considered and perhaps arranged new features and renovated existing ones, such as an ornamental pool, rock garden and dry retaining walls. Now you will be anxious to get under way with final ground preparation and replanting.

PREPARING AND IMPROVING SOIL

I cannot stress too strongly that the work of preparation should not be skimped: the more thoroughly it is done, the more rapid and successful will be the establishment and growth of your plants.

Soil will be poor and lacking in nutrients if for many years it has grown trees, shrubs and roses with little or no feeding. Assuming areas have been cleared of weed, stumps and tree roots, the next step is to add manure or compost. Well rotted farmyard manure from a local farm is ideal; failing this, a bagged equivalent from your nearest garden centre is excellent but expensive; well made garden compost or leafmould or composted seaweed (if you are near the sea) or a mixture of these will also give much needed humus and fertility to an impoverished soil, such as one over gravel sand or chalk. Spread a generous layer of manure or compost 2–3 in. (5–8 cm) thick (or as recommended by the supplier of bagged patent manure) and rotovate or hand-dig the planting area thoroughly, incorporating the manure as deeply as possible. If the area is small, hand-digging to a depth of at least 1½ ft (45 cm) is to be preferred, spading the manure to the bottom of the trench as the work proceeds. Allow the disturbed land to settle properly before planting. The earlier in the autumn this preparation can be carried out, the better; in particular, heavy clay soils rough-dug in the autumn will greatly benefit from the action of frost.

It is not always possible to remove roots of long-established trees and shrubs and these will compete strongly with new plants for available food and moisture. If planting space is limited, it may be

Ribes sanguineum 'Brocklebankii' will brighten up a shady corner. It has pink flowers in spring followed by black fruits

advisable to cut back the roots and seal off any subsequent root-growth with a reasonably long-lasting barrier of heavy gauge polythene or not-too-rusty sheets of corrugated iron, inserted as deeply as possible into the ground – about 3 ft (1 m) deep is best if ambitious. This should prevent the roots from reinvading the prepared and manured area for long enough to allow establishment of the new plants. The same technique can be practised where borders are impoverished by the hungry roots of hedges, especially privet and Leyland cypress.

PURCHASING TOP SOIL

Top soil is often essential when refurbishing a neglected garden, for replenishing a herbaceous border, rose bed or rock garden, but it can be a very variable product. It may be offered from road widening or building sites and a variety of other sources; it may be substantially chalky, gravelly or sandy and is frequently laced with roots of couch grass, bracken or bindweed, not to speak of bricks, lumps of concrete and every sort of industrial garbage.

If there are sand- or gravel-pits or stone-quarries within reasonable distance, it is worth enquiring there for good-quality top soil, which may be removed with turf and stockpiled before the gravel or stone is extracted. Whatever the source, do inspect and approve before the material is loaded; once delivered and tipped, it is usually too late!

DEALING WITH BADLY DRAINED AREAS

Badly drained areas will show up in times of heavy rain, when pools of water collect on a lawn or border. First, you should determine the nature and depth of your soil and subsoil. Old neglected gardens often suffer from layers of compacted soil or 'hard pan', which may have been caused by many years of shallow digging to the same depth, or by buried pathways or foundations of long-demolished buildings. All these factors will inhibit natural drainage on an otherwise free-draining soil. Systematic deep digging or forking through a badly drained patch may be enough to relieve the condition.

On heavy or clay soils, bad drainage is inevitable and if holes are dug in winter for planting, they tend to fill with water, creating a well or sump. In such circumstances, the planting pit should be mole- or land-drained to a ditch or soakaway at a lower point in the garden. Mound-planting 6 in. (15 cm) proud of the general level will also help and should be the rule for all beds and borders in badly drained gardens. However, if land-drains or mole-draining are ineffective or the problem is extensive, seek advice from a local drainage expert, who should be familiar with the soil and situation.

PLANTING

In prepared borders bare-rooted trees and shrubs should be planted by mid- to the end of March and preferably earlier, but choose open weather with the soil in a workable condition. Take out a generous hole in the dug and prepared ground and drive in a stake if necessary (see below); spread the roots of the plant evenly without cramping; then add planting compost at the rates advised on the bag to your heap of excavated local soil and mix well before back-filling the hole. Bagged tree and shrub planting compost, available from most garden centres, should contain all necessary nutrients, but moist peat or pulverized bark, in conjunction with a slow-release fertilizer, can be used instead. It is best to have an assistant to ensure that the plant is positioned at the correct level in relation to the previous soil – mark on the stem (a stout cane or spare spade laid across the hole will help here). The assistant can also gently shake the tree or shrub to allow soil to filter between the root fibres as back-filling proceeds. Firm in bare-root trees and

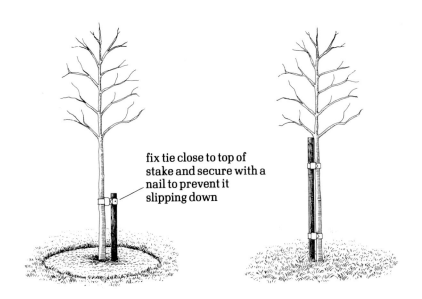

fix tie close to top of
stake and secure with a
nail to prevent it
slipping down

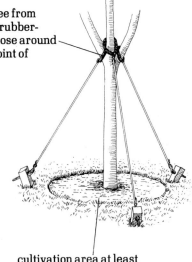

to protect tree from
damage use rubber-
reinforced hose around
hawser at point of
contact

Above left: Preferred method of
staking standard or feathered
trees

Above right: Incorrect staking
will result in a weak stem and
wounding by abrasion with the
top of the stake

Right: Guying an extra heavy
standard or semi-mature tree of
16 ft (5 m) or more

cultivation area at least
3 ft (1 m) in diameter

43

shrubs very thoroughly so that there is close contact between soil and roots and no air pockets. Finally, water in well to settle the soil about the roots and apply a 2 in. (5 cm) deep mulch of pulverized or ornamental-grade bark to conserve moisture and suppress weeds.

Isolated sites in turf or rough grass The larger the cultivation area, the better will be the establishment and subsequent growth of a tree or shrub which would otherwise have to compete for food and moisture with mown or rough grass. In such difficult circumstances it is recommended that tree sites are prepared as above, a minimum of 4 ft (1.2 m) wide cultivated to 2 ft (60 cm) deep; a minimum of 3 ft (1 m) wide and 1½ ft (45 cm) deep for shrubs. Watering, mulching and keeping these cultivated areas free from invading grass and weeds are particularly important.

Staking and securing for feathered and standard trees and large shrubs, will be necessary to stabilize the roots and lower part of the stem and aid establishment. Use stout, natural, pointed stakes 2–3 in. (5–8 cm) in diameter, tannilized or treated with a wood preservative which is harmless to plant life. If possible, drive in the stake at least 2 ft (60 cm) into the ground to make it firm; wood preservative should show at least 6 in. (15 cm) above the finished level. In accordance with recent research, I recommend that feathered or standard trees are provided with a basal stake no higher than 2–3 ft (60 cm–1 m) above ground level, secured with a purpose-made tree tie positioned at the very top of the stake and retained there by a nail passed through the strapping to prevent slipping down. This last point is often overlooked, with the result that serious wounding is caused to the stem by abrasion in the wind with the top of the stake. If this is neglected for even a few weeks, the stem can snap at this point in the next gale.

Heavy or semi-mature trees above about 10 ft (3 m) in height may require double staking to a greater height or, for the largest specimens, the use of hawser guys, with the tree protected by reinforced rubber hose and the guys secured at the base to short stakes of preserved wood driven at an angle towards the tree. Ideally, each guy should be provided with U-bolts at top and bottom and turnbuckles to ensure correct tension.

Container-grown and root-balled (usually evergreen) trees, shrubs and plants have the advantage of an extended season of planting: indeed, installation from containers is possible at almost any time of year as the plant should receive the minimum of disturbance.

Field-dug, root-balled evergreens should be planted by the end of April, with no more than the careful removal of hessian or plastic covers and, of course, the addition of planting compost, plus thorough firming, watering and mulching as for bare-root plants. The majority of container plants are commercially grown in peat- or bark-based composts, which are in sharp contrast to the soils of most gardens. To help the plant adapt, it is advisable to mix bagged planting compost or peat, bark and slow-release fertilizer as generously as you can afford with the surrounding soil before planting and back-filling.

Failure with otherwise healthy container-grown plants can frequently be traced to lack of moisture at the roots. At whatever season of planting, do ensure that the pot of soil is thoroughly moist throughout before it is set in the ground. As a general guide, unexpected lightness in weight in comparison to other moist plants will indicate dryness even, if the top surface is wet. In these circumstances (or if in doubt), plunge the pot in a bucket of water until the bubbles stop. Container plants which are planted dry tend to remain so and are likely to die in the next spring or summer drought. Again, a bark mulch will help establishment and growth and reduce maintenance.

If you wish to use a coarse grade of peat or an ornamental grade of bark as a soil-conditioner when planting trees, shrubs, roses and herbaceous plants, add a slow- or controlled-release fertilizer for the best results; equally, any of the prepacked rose fertilizers are excellent and need not be confined to roses. If you want to be strictly organic, then blood, fish and bone or bonemeal will serve you well. All these products will encourage root development and healthy growth. Subsequently, an annual spring dressing with one of them will sustain good balanced growth towards maturity.

Plants to Refurnish the Neglected Garden

To assist you in deciding what to use in association with existing shrubs, some resited, here is a short descriptive list of good garden shrubs, herbaceous plants and ground coverers, followed by plants for particular situations such as patios and pools. I have tended to concentrate on shrubs as they are so important to the permanent structure or 'bones' of the refurbished garden. Although well known, old favourites are mentioned, I have included a number of first-class recent introductions, which are less likely to be present in older gardens. All should be currently commercially available, or likely to be in the near future, but a recent edition of *The Plant Finder* should be consulted if you find it difficult to locate them (p. 64).

MEDIUM TO LARGE SHRUBS

These shrubs are useful for background planting, hedges or hedge reinforcement, screening and as specimens. M = medium-growing, 5–10 ft (1.5–3 m); L = large-growing, 10–13 ft + (3–4 m).

Aucuba japonica (M) Reliable, large-leaved, hardy and shade-tolerant evergreens of rounded habit; some variegated forms known as spotted laurel; females have large red berries. Distinct cultivars include: 'Crotonifolia' – leaves boldly speckled gold (female); 'Picturata' – leaves with prominent yellow central splash (male); 'Salicifolia' – large narrow leaves, very free-fruiting.

Berberis Large genus of deciduous and evergreen shrubs for sun or shade and most soils; yellow or orange flowers in spring; showy autumn berries and colouring leaves. B. gagnepainii (M) – makes an impenetrable hedge, black berries. B. 'Goldilocks' (valdiviana × darwinii) (L) – a promising new hybrid with dark glossy leaves and hanging red-stalked flower clusters. B. julianae (L) – a sturdy, dense screening shrub; young leaves copper-tinted. B. × stenophylla (M) – arching habit, spectacular flower in April. B. verruculosa (M) – neat and compact, another excellent hedge plant, with dark glossy leaves white beneath. All the above are evergreen.

Buddleia Unsurpassed for scented summer flowers; choose a sunny site; both deciduous. B. alternifolia (L) – graceful arching habit, narrow leaves and profuse lilac-coloured flowers in June. B. 'Lochinch' (fallowiana ×

davidii) (M) – a robust shrub, young grey leaves, later green above and white-felted beneath; large panicles of violet-blue flowers with orange eyes.

Buxus sempervirens (L) Common box, an invaluable native evergreen thriving in sun or shade; clippable as a dense hedge, formal or informal, and much used for topiary specimens. 'Elegantissima' – silver-variegated and a striking if slow growing, dome-shaped specimen.

Camellia × williamsii (M) Much loved, early spring flowering, hardy, evergreen shrubs for acid soil; site facing north or west. Among a host of cultivars 'Donation' remains supreme, with its delicately veined, semi-double, pink flowers and vigorous erect habit; also try 'E.T.R. Carlyon' – nearly double, white, late-flowering and often missing the frosts.

Ceanothus thyrsiflorus (L) A tall evergreen shrub to screen a south- or west-facing fence or for a wall; pale blue flowers in May and June; the hardiest of the Californian lilacs. *C.* 'Cascade' is similar, with arching growths and powder-blue flowers in panicles.

Cotinus (L) Smoke trees, popular both for foliage (deciduous) and for plume-like inflorescences in summer. I recommend: *C. coggygria* 'Flame' – orange autumn colour and pink plumes; 'Royal Purple' – leaves deep rich purple turning crimson in autumn; and 'Grace' – an exciting new hybrid, large-growing and vigorous, its large leaves red-purple with a grey sheen.

Cotoneaster A large and variable genus; white spring flowers and autumn berries; the evergreens are useful as fast-growing screens and for hedging. *C. conspicuus* 'Highlight' (M) – small leaves, orange-red fruits and arching habit. *C.* 'Exburiensis' (L) – large, pale green, lance-like leaves and yellow pink-tinted fruits. *C. franchetii var. sternianus* (L) – grey-green leaves and orange-red fruits. *C. lacteus* (M) – largish, leathery, oval leaves, grey beneath, and small red berries which ripen late and persist to New Year; an excellent informal hedger or screen for a north- or east-facing fence. All the above are evergreen.

Daphne bholua 'Jacqueline Postill' (M) Magnificent, new, upright-growing, hardy evergreen; fragrant mauve flowers, white within, from December to March; a superb specimen for loamy free-draining soil.

Elaeagnus (L) Fast-growing, wind-tolerant, large-leaved shrubs thriving on most fertile well-drained soils; the evergreens (as here) are very useful for screening or reinforcing hedges and several are attractively variegated; deliciously fragrant, autumn flowers hang like small parchment-coloured lanterns. *E. × ebbingei* 'Gilt Edge' – leaves with golden margins; 'Limelight' – central yellow blotch to the leaves, vigorous. *E. macrophylla* – has roundish silvery leaves and is perhaps the most reliable of the genus. *E. pungens* 'Gold Rim' – bright yellow margins to the leaves, vigorous and reliable.

Escallonia (M) Vigorous, evergreen, summer-flowering shrubs suitable for informal heges and screening. *E.* 'Donard Radiance' – densely bushy, with rich pink flowers; 'Donard Seedling' – arching growth, good for concealing a south- or west-facing fence, and white pink-flushed flowers. *E.* 'Crimson

Left: The glowing foliage of *Cotinus* 'Grace' associates well with silver-leaved plants (see p. 47)
Right: *Photinia* × *fraseri* 'Red Robin' is a large shrub for most fertile soils and notable for its persistent red shoots

Spire' – fast-growing and upright, with deep red flowers, an excellent hedger.

Genista aetnensis (L) The Mount Etna Broom, an elegant fast-growing, golden, July-flowering, deciduous shrub.

Ilex (L) The evergreen hollies are among the handsomest of all hardy, large shrubs or small trees and make excellent screeners, hedgers and reinforcers; female plants need a near-by male to produce berries. There are many superb variegated cultivars: *I.* × *altaclerensis* 'Golden King' (female) – broad-leaved, nearly spineless; 'Maderensis Variegata' (male) – very large leaves with central golden splash, makes a striking specimen. *I. aquifolium* 'Ferox Argentea' (male) – the silver variegated form of the prickly hedgehog holly; 'J.C. van Tol' – quite the most free-fruiting holly (perhaps hermaphrodite), an excellent hedge plant with few spines.

Kolkwitzia amabilis 'Pink Cloud' (L) Beauty bush, a very hardy, graceful arching, deciduous shrub, with peeling winter bark and a great display of pink foxglove-like flowers in early summer.

Mahonia Shade-tolerant evergreens with pinnate holly-like leaves and yellow winter or spring flowers. *M. aquifolium* 'Atropurpurea' (M) – dark purple-red winter leaves, a useful small specimen or hedge reinforcement. *M. japonica* (M) – without doubt one of the most worthwhile of all hardy shrubs, elegant in habit, magnificent in foliage at all seasons and having large, lax, terminal racemes of lily-of-the-valley-scented flowers during winter. *M. pinnata* (M) – a strong-growing dense, prickly evergreen, with clusters of rich yellow flowers freely produced in late winter; its hybrid 'Undulata' (M) has lustrous leaves with wavy margins.

Osmanthus (M) Handsome, hardy, holly-like evergreens, useful as specimens or for hedges. *O.* × *burkwoodii* (× *Osmarea burkwoodii*) – excellent, dense, bushy evergreen, fragrant white flowers in April. *O. heterophyllus* 'Aureomarginatus' – tough, spine-toothed, yellow-margined leaves; 'Gulftide' – curiously lobed and twisted spiny leaves and a dense habit, fragrant white flowers in autumn.

Photinia Both the following evergreen shrubs are hardy in sheltered circumstances, tolerant of alkaline (limy) soils and rival the acid-soil-loving *Pieris* in the brilliance and persistence of their young red foliage; useful hedge reinforcers and screeners. *P. glabra* 'Rubens' (M) – forms a dense shrub with leathery leaves which are sealing-wax red for many weeks when young. *P.* × *fraseri* 'Red Robin' (L) has larger leaves and bright red shoots and leaves.

Pieris japonica (M) Evergreen, rounded, bushy shrub with glossy, dark green foliage; drooping racemes of white flowers in spring may be damaged by frost; needs a sheltered spot and acid soil. Cultivars have bronze or red young foliage and some have pink flowers. *P.* 'Forest Flame' (L) – vivid red young leaves, shading to pink, cream and finally dark green, with white flowers.

Rhododendron Hardy Hybrids (M) Of this immense, diverse and much loved family, it is perhaps best for the non-specialist to choose from the many well tried cultivars suitable for general background plantings; for acid soil only; some shade is preferable. The following give a range of flower colour from April (early) to the end of June (late): 'Bagshot Ruby' – ruby-red, vigorous (mid); 'Betty Wormald' – deep rose-pink with crimson markings (mid); 'Boddaertianum' (L) – tall-growing, vigorous, lavender-blue (early); 'Elizabeth' – mound-forming to 5 ft (1.5 m), deep pure red (early); 'Goldsworth Yellow' – apricot-pink buds opening primrose-yellow (mid-late); 'Gower Waterer' – a large bush, white flushed mauve (mid-late); 'Pink Pearl' – strong and tall, deep lilac-pink (mid); 'Purple Splendour' – deep purple-blue, blends well with 'Goldsworth Yellow' (mid-late).

Viburnum Easily cultivated shrubs providing us with some of the most desirable woody plants for our gardens. *V.* × *burkwoodii* (M) – dark shining evergreen leaves and fragrant, pink-budded, white flowers from February to May, good for hedge reinforcement. *V. opulus* 'Roseum' ('Sterile') (L) – snowball-like creamy-white flower heads in summer, a spectacular, hardy, deciduous shrub. *V. plicatum* 'Lanarth' (M) – stronger in growth and less horizontally branched than the more frequently planted 'Mariesii' (M), which is better as an isolated specimen; deciduous, both have a profusion of creamy white, flat flower heads in May and June and good autumn leaf colour. *V.* 'Pragense' (*rhytidophyllum* × *utile*) (L) – a very hardy evergreen deserving wider planting, lustrous, dark green leaves white-felted beneath and creamy white flowers in May. *V. tinus* (M) – laurustinus, an invaluable winter flowering evergreen for hedges; *V. tinus*

A superb combination of evergreens: cool variegated *Euonymus* 'Emerald Gaiety' backed by *Mahonia japonica* with a purple berberis to the right

'Eve Price', compact habit and pink-tinted buds, is an excellent cultivar and ideal to screen a north- or east-facing fence.

DWARF AND SMALL COMPACT SHRUBS

These shrubs may be used in middle distance and foreground planting, in island beds and to add height to ground cover. D = dwarf, 1–3 ft (30–90 cm); S = small, 3–5 ft (1–1.5 m).

Cotoneaster salicifolius 'Gnom' (D) Prostrate evergreen with red berries.

Cytisus *C.* × *beanii* (D) Golden yellow flowers. *C.* × *kewensis* – semi-prostrate, cream flowers. Both deciduous.

Daphne × **burkwoodii** (S) Semi-evergreen with fragrant, pale pink flowers in May and June. *D. tangutica* (D) – evergreen with fragrant, white, purple-tinted flowers in March and April.

Euonymus 'Emerald Gaiety' (S), silver-variegated, and 'Emerald 'n' Gold' (D), golden-variegated evergreen leaves.

Fuchsia 'Lady Thumb' (D) Deciduous shrub with red and white flowers in summer and autumn. *F. magellanica* 'Versicolor' (S) – grey-green, cream and pink variegated leaves. Deciduous and hardy once established.

Genista tinctoria 'Royal Gold' (S) Golden yellow flowers throughout summer; deciduous.

Hebe salicifolia 'Spender's Seedling' (S) Evergreen narrow leaves, white flowers all summer.

Hydrangea *H. arborescens* 'Annabelle' (S) Spectacular, round, white flower heads in summer and autumn. *H. serrata* 'Preziosa' (S) – pink flowers, purple-tinted leaves. Both deciduous.

Perovskia atriplicifolia 'Blue Spire' (S) Lavender-blue flowers in late summer.

Pieris japonica 'Little Heath' (S) Evergreen with coppery young growths, white spring flowers, for acid soil.

Potentilla 'Day Dawn' (S), peach-pink, and 'Tangerine' (D), orange flowers in summer and autumn; semi-shade desirable, both deciduous.

Rhododendron 'Blue Tit' (S) – lavender-blue flowers in May. *R. yakushimanum* (S) – pink in bud, opening white; unsurpassed in foliage and flower. *R.* 'Surrey Heath' (S) – a rose-pink *yakushimanum* hybrid. *R.* 'Blaauw's Pink' and 'Palestrina' (S) – azaleas in salmon-pink and white. All evergreen and needing acid soil.

Foliage effect

Grey, white and silver
Artemisia 'Powis Castle' (S, evergreen)
Hebe colensoi 'Glauca' (D, evergreen)
H. pimeloides 'Quick Silver' (D, evergreen)
Helichrysum italicum (D, evergreen)
H. splendidum (S, evergreen)
Phlomis fruticosa (S, evergreen)
Salix lanata (S)
Santolina chamaecyparissus var. *nana* (var. *corsica*) (D, evergreen)

Purple and red
Acer palmatum 'Dissectum Crimson Queen' (S) – give shade and shelter
Berberis thunbergii 'Atropurpurea Nana' (D); 'Red Chief' (S)
Mahonia aquifolium 'Atropurpurea' (S, evergreen)
Nandina domestica 'Nana Purpurea' (S, evergreen)

Yellow and golden – all best in a little shade
Berberis thunbergii 'Aurea' (S)
Choisya ternata 'Sundance' (S, evergreen)
Lonicera nitida 'Baggesen's Gold' (S, evergreen)
Physocarpus opulifolius 'Dart's Gold' (S)
Ribes sanguineum 'Brocklebankii' (S)
Spiraea × *bumalda* (*S. japonica*) 'Goldflame' (D)

GROUND COVER

Herbaceous plants

These are some reliable hardy herbaceous perennials for ground cover and others to associate with shrubs. They are grouped according to their preferences and most are of average vigour of

Left: For a pool of glowing yellow foliage in a shaded spot plant
Physocarpus opulifolius 'Dart's Gold'
Right: *Alchemilla mollis* is an extremely useful groundcoverer for the front
of a border, with herbs or beneath roses

spread, unless otherwise stated. M = medium, 2–3 ft (60–90 cm);
S = small, 1–2 ft (30–60 cm); D = dwarf, 6–8 in (15–20 cm); VD = very
dwarf, under 6–8 in. (15 cm).

Sun

Agapanthus Headbourne Hybrids (M) Blue flowers August-September,
clump-forming. Select a well drained site.

Aster frikartii (M) Blue flowers with orange eye autumn, clump-forming.

Dianthus 'Mrs Sinkins' (D) A border pink with double, white fragrant
flowers May–June.

Diascia 'Ruby Field' (D) Showy pink flowers all summer.

Gypsophila paniculata 'Rosy Veil' (S) Grey leaves, double pink flowers
summer.

Sedum 'Autumn Joy' (S) Fleshy leaves, flowers pink tinted bronze
September–October; clump-forming 'Ruby Glow' (D) – purple-tinted
leaves, ruby-red flowers.

Sun or semi-shade

Alchemilla mollis (S) Beautiful foliage, green-yellow flowers summer.

Viola cornuta (D) Horned viola, with clear blue flowers May–August.
'Alba' – white.

Waldsteinia ternata (VD) Evergreen carpet with yellow flowers
April–May.

Left: *Dicentra eximea* 'Luxurians' in full flower and displaying its attractive fern-like foliage
Right: *Heuchera* 'Palace Purple' is an unusual foliage plant for a semi-shady situation. It combines well with pale green or grey

Semi-shade or shade

Anemone × hybrida (M) Japanese anemone, 'Queen Charlotte', pink single, and 'White Queen', single, August–October.

Bergenia 'Ballawley' (S) Large evergreen leaves, red in winter, rose-pink flowers spring. 'Silberlicht' ('Silver Light') – white and pale pink flowers.

Brunnera macrophylla (S) Large heart-shaped leaves, forget-me-not blue flowers June. 'Variegata' – cream-mottled leaves.

Cyclamen hederifolium (*C. neapolitanum*) (VD) Beautiful marbled leaves, pink flowers September–October, clump-forming. Var. *album* – white.

Dicentra eximea (S) 'Alba', white, and 'Luxurians', pink flowers late spring.

Epimedium × rubrum (S) Crimson flowers March–April, autumn leaf colour.

Euphorbia polychroma (M) Spurge, with bright yellow flowers early spring and autumn leaf colour; clump-forming.

Geranium *G. endressii* (S) 'A T Johnson', silvery pink, and 'Wargrave Pink', bright pink, summer. *G.* 'Johnson's Blue', deep lavender-blue, clump-forming. *G. macrorrhizum* 'Ingwersen's Variety' (S) – neat aromatic leaves, shell-pink flowers.

Heuchera 'Palace Purple' (M) Purple evergreen leaves and elegant white flower sprays all summer; clump-forming. A first-class newcomer.

Hosta 'August Moon' (M) Golden leaves. 'Halcyon' (S) – blue leaves. *H. lancifolia* (S) – narrow, dark green leaves, lavender-blue flowers early summer. And many others, all clump-forming.

Diascia 'Ruby Field' (see p. 52) will flower continuously through summer. It is a charming, fine-textured plant for a border and looks superb in a container, although dead heading will be required from time to time to keep the display going

Lamium maculatum 'Beacon Silver' (S) Pink flowers summer and silver leaves.

Liriope muscari (S) Evergreen grassy leaves, violet flower spikes September–October; clump-forming.

Lysimachia nummularia (VD) Creeping Jenny, with green leaves and golden flowers summer. 'Aurea' – golden leaves.

Ophiopogon planiscapus 'Nigrescens' (VD) Black-purple, grassy, evergreen foliage, white flowers late summer, then black berries; slow-growing and compact. Unusual.

Pulmonaria *P. angustifolia* 'Azurea' (D) Gentian-blue flowers March–April; good with our native primrose. *P. saccarata* 'Pink Dawn' (D) – leaves marbled white, pink flowers.

Shade

Ajuga reptans 'Burgundy Glow' (VD) Pink-, purple- and cream-variegated leaves. 'Atropurpurea' – deep purple leaves, blue flowers spring.

Campanula alliariifolia 'Ivory Bells' (S) Arching habit and long season of white flowers, clump-forming.

Helleborus *H. lividus* subsp. *corsicus argutifolius* (M) Evergreen leathery leaves, apple-green flowers winter, clump-forming. *H. orientalis* – Lenten rose, with white, pink or purple flowers January-March.

Iris foetidissima (S) Gladwyn iris, a shade-tolerant native evergreen, with scarlet seed heads autumn and winter; clump-forming. 'Variegata' – leaves with broad silver margins.

Left: *Liriope muscari*, a clump-forming perennial with bright green, glossy leaves, will add interest to a border with its autumn flowers
Right: *Helianthemum* 'Georgeham' is a neat groundcoverer for a sunny spot and it flourishes in limy soils

Shrubs

Heathers (*Erica*, *Calluna* and *Daboecia* – the last two for acid soils only) are much used as evergreen ground cover, notably between shrubs and dwarf conifers in island beds. (See *Wisley Handbook: Heaths and Heathers*.) Equally, the new ground-cover or landscape roses are enjoying great popularity and the number of excellent cultivars increases annually. They are ideal for sunny banks and at the top of dry retaining walls. I particularly admire 'Nozomi', pale pink; 'Red Max Graf,' scarlet; 'The Fairy', rose-pink; and 'Snow Carpet', white.

The following is a short list of reliable and readily available shrubby ground covers, which show considerable diversity in foliage, flower and berry. (For key, see p. 52.)

Sun

Ceratostigma plumbaginoides (D) Dwarf hardy plumbago, with blue flowers autumn and red foliage.
Helianthemum nummularium cultivars (D) Grey or green evergreen leaves, wide range of flower colour all summer.
Salvia officinalis (S) 'Icterina', variegated common sage and 'Purpurescens' with purple evergreen leaves.
Teucrium chamaedrys (D) Aromatic evergreen sub-shrub, rose-pink flowers July–September.

Left: Shade-loving *Cornus canadensis* is a woodland plant well-suited to growing beneath a tree
Right: The creeping stems of *Polygonum vacciniifolium* will spread to drape a retaining wall or soften paving at the edge of a border

Sun or shade

Cotoneaster dammeri (VD) Trailing evergreen with bright red berries.
Hebe pinguifolia 'Pagei' (D) Grey evergreen foliage and white flowers May; slow-growing and compact.
Pachysandra terminalis 'Variegata' (S) Very shade-tolerant evergreen with leaves white-variegated.
Vinca minor (VD) Lesser periwinkle, an evergreen with bright blue flowers intermittently spring to autumn. Good cultivars include 'Bowles' Variety', large azure-blue; 'Gertrude Jekyll', white; and 'Variegata', blue flowers, leaves variegated creamy white.

Shade

Cornus canadensis (*Chamaepericlymenum canadense*) (VD) Creeping dogwood, with white summer flowers and red berries; acid soil only.

PLANTS FOR PARTICULAR SITUATIONS

Mossy lawns

For moss-infested lawns, there are several appropriate and interesting plants of very low growth which can be planted as permanent ground cover to replace the grass. On a small scale, one can experiment with *Cotula squalida* and *Lysimachia nummularia* and its golden-leaved form (p. 54). In mild districts, *Pratia pedunculata* and *P. treadwelli* and *Soleirolia (Helxine) soleirolii* or mind-your-own-business, also found in a yellow-leaved form, could be tried. Some of the many cultivars available of *Hedera helix* or English ivy, including the variegated ones, are useful too. If the soil never dries out, the charming, native, creeping willows, *Salix herbacea* and *S. reticulata*, are possible, while on acid soils the tiny, prostrate, berrying evergreen, *Gaultheria procumbens*, colonizes well.

Dry-stone walls

Alpines
Aethionema – pink
Alyssum – yellow
Aubrieta-blue, violet, red, pink
Campanula portenschlagiana – blue
Corydalis lutea – yellow fumitory
Geranium sanguineum var. *striatum* (var. *lancastriense*) or *G. dalmaticum* – pink cranesbills
Gypsophila paniculata 'Rosy Veil' (p. 52)
Haberlea rhodopensis – blue, for shade
Helianthemum – sun roses
Iberis sempervirens – evergreen candytuft, white
Lewisia hybrids – pink
Phlox subulata cultivars
Polygonum vacciniifolium – pink
Ramonda myconi – blue, for shade
Saponaria ocymoides – rose-pink
Tunica saxifraga – pale pink
Zauschneria cana – scarlet

Shrubs and conifers – draping, mostly evergreen
Cotoneaster dammeri (p. 56)
Genista pilosa or *G. procumbens* – golden
Hedera helix 'Gold Heart' or 'Ivalace'
Juniperus procumbens 'Nana' or *J. horizontalis* 'Wiltonii'
Parahebe catarractae – pale blue
Roses – ground covering (p. 55)
Teucrium chamaedrys (p. 55)

Paved areas

Armeria juniperifolia (A. caespitosa) – pink; or *A. maritima* 'Vindictive' – red thrift
Campanula carpatica cultivars – dwarf compact bellflowers
Dianthus 'La Bourboule' ('La Bourbrille') or *D. deltoides* cultivars – pinks

Hebe 'Boughton Dome' – blue-green evergreen leaves; or *H. pinguifolia* 'Pagei' (p. 56)
Hypericum olympicum or the cultivar 'Citrinum' – low-growing St John's worts
Origanum vulgare 'Aureum' – golden marjoram
Saxifraga 'Pixie' – mossy saxifrage; or *S.* × *urbium* 'Primuloides' – dainty London Pride; both best with some shade
Silene shafta – rose-red autumn-flowering campion
Teucrium ackermanii – a grey-leaved aromatic germander, purple-red flowers
Thymus × *drucei* (*T. serpyllum*) – pink, crimson or white; the best scented thyme for paving and a British native
Veronica prostrata – a vivid blue speedwell

Ornamental pools

Here are some excellent shallow-water or marginal aquatic plants, of moderate or clump-forming growth, which are hardy and effective in flower and foliage from spring to autumn and suitable for small garden pools. (For key, see p. 52.)

Acorus calamus 'Variegatus' (M), variegated sweet flag
Caltha palustris 'Flore Pleno' (S), double marsh marigold
Carex riparia 'Bowles' Golden' (S), golden rush
Iris laevigata (M), Japanese water iris
Lobelia cardinalis (M) scarlet flowers – lift and store frost-free in winter
Mentha aquatica (M), water mint – lilac-coloured flowers
Mimulus luteus (S), yellow musk
Pontederia cordata (S), pickerel – blue flowers
Sagittaria sagittifolia (S), arrow head – white flowers with black eyes
Sparganium ramosum (M), bur-reed – green flowers and seeds heads
Typha minima (M), dwarf reedmace
Veronica beccabunga (D), brooklime – blue flowers
Water lilies of moderate growth – up to 3 ft (1 m) spread of leaves: *Nymphaea* 'Odorata Alba', white, scented; 'Escarboucle', crimson; 'Graziella', deep apricot; 'James Brydon', rose-red; 'Odorata Sulphurea' yellow, scented; 'Princess Elizabeth', pink

Plans

Descriptions of most of the plants included in the plans are given on pp. 46-58. Scales throughout are approximately 8 ft to 1 in (1:100).

FOCAL-POINT PLANTINGS

These schemes are designed for colour and interest at all seasons. Usually viewed from the house or patio, they are adaptable to small areas 25-30 ft (8-10 m) long by 10-14 ft (3-4.5 m) deep. They will often be sited against an existing shrub background, hedge, wall or fence, or these can be added if desired. Groups of daffodils, snowdrops and other spring bulbs may be interspersed among herbaceous ground coverers, especially hostas. * = evergreen.

North-facing

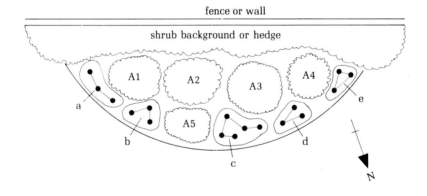

Key to plants

Herbaceous plants and ground covers
a = *Helleborus lividus* subsp. *corsicus** or *H. orientalis*
b = *Hosta* 'August Moon' or *H. fortunei* 'Albo-picta'
c = *Anemone* × *hybrida* 'Queen Charlotte' or 'White Queen'
d = *Hosta* 'Halcyon' or *H. lancifolia*
e = *Campanula alliarifolia* 'Ivory Bells' or *Iris foetidissima* 'Variegata'*

Shrubs

A1 = *Cotoneaster lacteus** or *C. franchetii* var. *sternianus**
A2 = *Camellia* × *williamsii* 'Donation'* (acid soil only) or *Daphne bholua* 'Jacqueline Postill'*
A3 = *Ilex* × *altaclerensis* 'Golden King'* (female) or 'Maderensis Variegata'* (male)
A4 = *Viburnum opulus* 'Roseum' ('Sterile') or *Hydrangea arborescens* 'Annabelle'
A5 = *Berberis thunbergii* 'Aurea'

South-facing

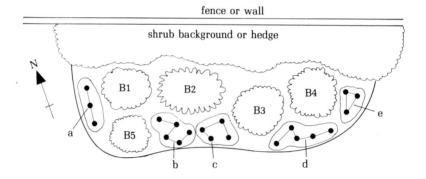

Key to plants

Herbaceous plants and ground coverers
a = *Viola cornuta* or cv. 'Alba'
b = *Teucrium chamaedrys**
c = *Agapanthus* Headbourne Hybrids
d = *Geranium macrorrhizum* 'Ingwersen's Variety'
e = *Euphorbia polychroma*

Shrubs

B1 = *Elaeagnus* × *ebbingei* 'Gilt Edge'* or *E. pungens* 'Gold Rim'*
B2 = *Buddleia alternifolia*
B3 = *Kolkwitzia amabilis* 'Pink Cloud' or *Genista aetnensis*
B4 = *Photinia* × *fraseri* 'Red Robin'* or *P. glabra* 'Rubens'*
B5 = *Perovskia atriplicifolia* 'Blue Spire'

ROSE GARDENS

Former sunken rose garden

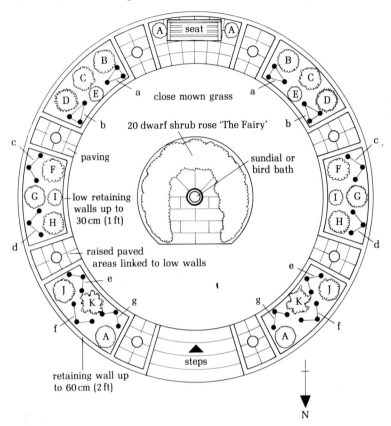

This circular design is refurnished with dwarf shrubs and associating plants to provide a matching arrangement for year-round effect in a sunny open situation.

Key to plants

Dwarf shrubs

A = *Buxus sempervirens* 'Elegantissima'*
B = *Lonicera nitida* 'Baggesen's Gold'*
C = *Helichrysum italicum* or *H. splendidum**
D = *Erica erigena* (*E.mediterranea*) 'Brightness'* or 'Irish Dusk'*
E = *Berberis thunbergii* 'Atropurpurea Nana' or 'Red Chief'
F = *Viburnum davidii**
G = *Choisya ternata* 'Sundance'* or *Spiraea × bumalda* (*S. japonica*) 'Goldflame'

H = *Euonymus* 'Emerald Gaiety'*
I = *Hebe pinguifolia* 'Quicksilver'* or 'Pagei'*
J = *Daphne* × *burkwoodii* or *D. tangutica**
K = *Cotoneaster salicifolius* 'Gnom'*

Herbaceous plants and ground covers

a = *Ceratostigma plumbaginoides*
b = *Viola cornuta*
c = *Anemone* × *hybrida* 'Queen Charlotte'
d = *Agapanthus* Headbourne Hybrids or *Aster* × *frikartii*
e = *Gypsophila paniculata* 'Rosy Veil'
f = *Sedum* 'Autumn Joy'
g = *Alchemilla mollis*

○ = urns or pots (these can be added to raised paved areas and flanking steps)

Former formal rose garden

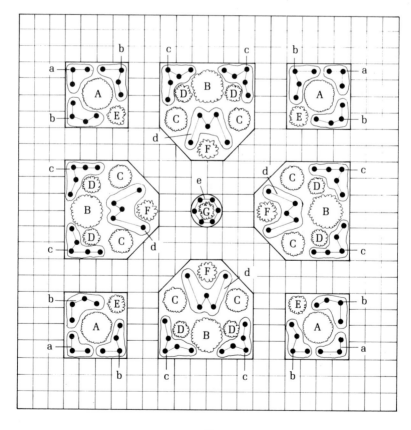

Hydrangea serrata 'Preziosa', planted here with a golden-leaved heath, screens a fence. A free-flowering cultivar with purple-tinted leaves

Set in paving, this is replanted with dwarf, predominantly evergreen shrubs and associated plants to give interest at all seasons in sun or semi-shade.

Key to plants

Dwarf shrubs
A = *Buxus sempervirens**
B = *Phlomis fruticosa** (sun) or *Salix lanata* (semi-shade)
C = *Choisya ternata* 'Sundance'*
D = *Euonymus* 'Emerald Gaiety'*
E = *Hebe colensoi* 'Glauca'*
F = *Hydrangea serrata* 'Preziosa'
G = *Cotoneaster* 'Hybridus Pendulus'* (standard)

Associated plants
a = *Santolina chamaecyparissus* var. *nana* (var. *corsica*)* or *Hebe pinguifolia* 'Pagei'*
b = *Geranium macrorrhizum* 'Ingwersen's Variety'
c = *Cotoneaster dammeri**
d = *Heuchera* 'Palace Purple'*
e = *Vinca minor* 'Variegata'*

Further Information

USEFUL ADDRESSES

Pathology Department, RHS Garden, Wisley, Woking, Surrey GU23 6QB. Tel. (0483) 224234. Advice and leaflet on honey fungus.

Agricultural Advisory Information Office, Forestry Commission Research Station, Alice Holt Lodge, Farnham, Surrey GU10 4LH. Tel. (0420) 22255. Arboricultural leaflet No.2 on honey fungus and leaflets on other diseases including phytophthora and fireblight.

HM Stationery Office Publications (mail and telephone orders only), PO Box 276, London SW8 5DT. Tel. 071-211-5656

Chempak Products Ltd (fertilizers and related products), Geddings Road, Hoddesdon, Herts EN11 OLR. Tel. (0992) 441888.

National Council for the Conservation of Plants and Gardens (NCCPG), The Pines, RHS Garden, Wisley (as above).

RECOMMENDED READING

A full list of Wisley Handbooks appears on the inside back cover and many will be particularly useful for those refurbishing a neglected garden including *Ground Cover Plants, Weed Control in the Garden* and *The Mixed Border*. In addition many helpful plans can be found in *Plans for Small Gardens* and *Plans for Small Gardens 2*.

The Hillier Book of Garden Planning and Planting, by Keith Rushforth, Roderick Griffin and Dennis Woodland (David & Charles 1988)

The Wisley Book of Gardening, edited by Robert Pearson (Collingridge 1981)

Rock Gardeners' Handbook, by Alan Titchmarsh (Croom Helm 1983)

The Plant Finder (The Hardy Plant Society, revised annually)